Children of the Gold Rush

Unknown little girl,
prepared for mining
in the North

CHILDREN

of the

GOLD RUSH

CLAIRE RUDOLF MURPHY
& JANE G. HAIGH

ROBERTS RINEHART PUBLISHERS
Boulder, Colorado

Published by
ROBERTS RINEHART PUBLISHERS
6309 Monarch Park Place
Niwot, Colorado 80503
www.robertsrinehart.com
A study guide is available from the publisher.

Distributed to the trade by Publishers Group West

Published in the UK and Ireland by
ROBERTS RINEHART PUBLISHERS
Trinity House, Charleston Road
Dublin 6, Ireland

Copyright © 1999 by Claire Rudolf Murphy & Jane G. Haigh

Cover and interior design and production:
Polly Christensen, Christensen & Son Design

Maps created and adapted for this book by
Marge Mueller, Gray Mouse Graphics

Map images excerpted from *Gold Rush Women*, by
Claire Rudolf Murphy and Jane G. Haigh, © 1997.
Reprinted with permission of Alaska Northwest Books.

International Standard Book Number 1-57098-257-0

Library of Congress Catalog Card Number 98-88245

10 9 8 7 6 5 4 3 2

Manufactured in Canada by Printcrafters

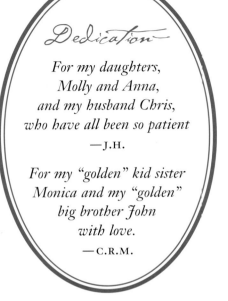

Dedication

For my daughters,
Molly and Anna,
and my husband Chris,
who have all been so patient
—J.H.

For my "golden" kid sister
Monica and my "golden"
big brother John
with love.
—C.R.M.

CONTENTS

ACKNOWLEDGMENTS

WE COULD NOT HAVE COMPLETED this book without the assistance of many individuals over the last five years. These include Candy Waugaman; authors Frances Backhouse, Mike Gates, Melanie Mayer, Dave Neufeld, and Frank Norris; George Harper of the Blacks in Alaska history project; Doreen Cooper, Project Archeologist at the Klondike Gold Rush National Historic Park in Skagway; archeologist and historian Bob King; Athabascan anthropologists Phyllis Fast and Miranda Wright, and Effie Kokrine, who helped us understand Athabascan culture and history; Barbara Nelson and her Mayo family relatives; Judy Grimes, Klondy Nelson's granddaughter, and Cleora Casady's granddaughters Donna Rankin and Jeanette Schlerith; historian John Cook, Pat Partnow, Mary Warren, and Lee Alder, for their information about the Cherosky family; historian Terrence Cole; and Mining Professor Emeritus Earl Beistline of the University of Alaska, for reviewing the gold mining material.

The Alaskana collection at the Rasmuson Library, University of Alaska Fairbanks, and the staff of the Alaska and Polar Regions Department have been unfailingly hospitable. We thank all of the staff, including director Susan Griggs, archivist Gretchen Lake, Marge Heath, Ron Inouye, Sylvie Savage, Rose Speranza and Robyn Russell. Thanks also to the research staff at the Noel Wein Library in Fairbanks, including Marjorie Cole, Sue Sherif,and Greg Hill; to Jane Williams, the late Pat Oakes, and the staff of the Circle District Historical Society and Museum; the staff of the Yukon Archives in Whitehorse; Kay Shelton and staff at the Alaska State Library; Diane Brenner at the Anchorage Museum of History and Art; the Dawson City Museum in Dawson; Elva Scott of the Eagle Historical Society; and Terry Dickey, Wanda Chin and Mollie Lee at the University of Alaska Museum; Ken DeRoux at the Alaska State Museum, and Mary Pat Wyatt at the Juneau City Museum.

INTRODUCTION

Leaves on the nearby trees were turning yellow and a chilly wind blew through the gold camp. Ten-year-old Donald McDonald watched the miners shovel the pay-dirt into the wooden sluice boxes. When the miners stopped the water flowing through the boxes, Donald's father motioned him over. Dipping both hands in the freezing liquid, Donald felt around in the gravel and sand at the bottom. Suddenly, up came his fingers, clutching shiny nuggets. "Gold!" he screamed. "Look, Mama, I'm rich!" The miners and prospectors laughed. They wanted to get rich, too—and some of them did.

One hundred years ago scenes like these were repeated throughout the Yukon and the Alaska territories, wherever gold was being mined. In America and around the world people had lost their jobs and were suffering through a great economic depression. So when news arrived about gold discoveries in the North country, thousands of men and women traveled there to seek their fortune. As a result, many children grew up in these gold rush settlements.

Some children came North with their mothers to join long-absent fathers. Others were born in the new boomtowns. Many were members of Native Alaskan or Yukon First Nations bands who had lived in the North for thousands of years. The lives of these Native people changed forever when gold rushers settled where only family fish camps had existed before. Some children had Native mothers and white fathers, arrangements that were common and practical early in the settlement of the North. As these children grew up, they had to choose between the new world of mining and towns, and the traditional Native lifestyle of fishing, trapping and hunting.

Gold was first discovered in the Yukon in 1886. But only a few hundred people came North until the Klondike River discoveries sparked the great gold rush of 1897–1898. For the next twenty-five years, thousands of gold seekers poured into Skagway, Dyea, Dawson, Nome, Fairbanks, Rampart, Iditarod, Livengood and dozens of other boomtowns.

To get to the new goldfields, pioneers

traveled North by ship up Alaska's Inside Passage. Travel took weeks and food and accommodations were poor. Those landing in Skagway began a 32-mile hike up and over the treacherous White Pass Trail or the rugged Chilkoot Trail from nearby Dyea. Then they had to float 600 miles downstream to Dawson City. Many people gave up before they even reached their destination.

Some traveled by ship all the way to St. Michael, then had to board a riverboat for the next 1500-mile trip upstream to Dawson. Travelers who arrived after the White Pass Railroad was constructed in 1899 could take the train from Skagway to Whitehorse, then steamship to Dawson. People heading to the new gold rush of Nome in 1900 took a ship all the way. Later in 1903–1904, goldrushers heading to Fairbanks took a boat to Valdez and then horse-drawn sled up the 500-mile Valdez trail. No matter which route they took, the journey was long and torturous. The kids who endured these expeditions were just as hardy as the adults were, and they gave hope to all their fellow travelers. When they finally arrived, even the toughest of pioneers, young or old, were challenged by the mosquito-filled summers and cold, dark winters.

In every new boomtown, goldseekers and entrepreneurs pitched canvas tents and built log buildings on muddy streets. Then someone would start a sawmill, and soon the new streets would sport false-fronted businesses and board sidewalks. Out on the gold creeks, families crowded together in tiny cabins.

Native people and early prospectors taught both parents and children about survival in the North. They learned how to pick berries, build cabins, and cut spruce boughs for soft bedding. Gold rush kids learned to eat new foods such as moose, caribou, and rabbit stew, dried salmon, and sourdough pancakes. When temperatures dropped below zero, they bundled up in fur clothing to play outside in the few short hours of winter daylight. In summertime they played outdoors all night because the sun never set.

If the children were fortunate enough to have a school, they often had no reading or arithmetic books. Instead, they might read pages torn from magazines, and use chalk slates to do their figures. White children went to school side by side with the Native children, sometimes learning their traditional language. For some children, there was no school at all, so they had their lessons at home. Native or immigrant, they learned the value of education and a surprising number later attended college.

Although everyone who searched for gold hoped to get rich, few people actually did. Fathers and mothers spent long hours working. Many children worked as well,

Children of the Gold Rush

baking bread, selling newspapers, sewing, or picking blueberries to sell. Learning to work hard at a very young age may have been their best lesson of all.

Many children overcame difficult family circumstances. Separation and divorce were common in the often confusing gold rush world of travel, change, and greed. Brave and full of adventure, gold rush kids quickly learned how to adapt and make the most of their new situations. And perhaps infected by the eternal optimism of the goldseekers, they learned to be positive, even during times of misfortune.

Some gold rush kids stayed only a few short years, but they never forgot their experiences. Others grew up to work at steady jobs and raise their own children in an Alaska that had changed dramatically since their childhood.

The children featured in this book represent the variety of adventures that gold rush kids experienced a hundred years ago. Gold rush kids were entertainers like Crystal and Monte Snow, Native children of prospectors like the Cherosky sisters, shortime visitors joining their papas like the Anderson children, and a military "brat" like Robert Farnsworth. Some were children of mixed marriages like the Mayo twins, a little girl in search of her papa like Klondy Nelson, a child of divorce like Cleora Casady, and

a young entrepreneur, more successful than his father, like Donald McDonald.

A hundred years later, we know about these remarkable children because of the records they left. Some wrote about their adventures in books or magazines. Others left behind their unpublished diaries and poems. Still others passed on their rich memories to their descendants who have shared them with us.

Throngs of people crowd the docks in Seattle to watch the steamer *Ohio* embark for the gold rush.

SOME TRAIL HINTS

❖ Don't waste a single ounce of anything, even if you don't like it. Put it away, and it will come in handy when you do like it.

❖ Don't eat ice or snow. Go thirsty until you can melt it.

❖ No man can continuously drag more than his own weight. Remember that this is a fact.

❖ Keep ypour sleeping bag clean. If it becomes inhabited, freeze the inhabitants out.

❖ A little dry grass or hay in the inside of your mitts, next to your hands, will promote great heat.

❖ When your nose is bitterly cold, stuff both nostrils with fur, cotton, or wool.

❖ There are no snakes in Alaska.

❖ Don't catch hold of your gun barrel when 30 degrees below zero is registered. Watch out for getting snow in the barrel. If you do, don't shoot it out.

(above) Trail hints from a list widely distributed at the time of the gold rush

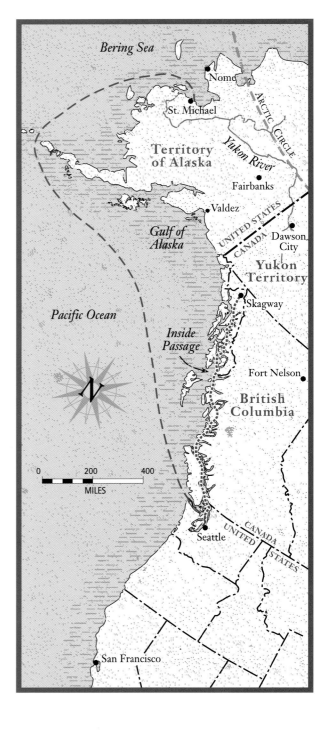

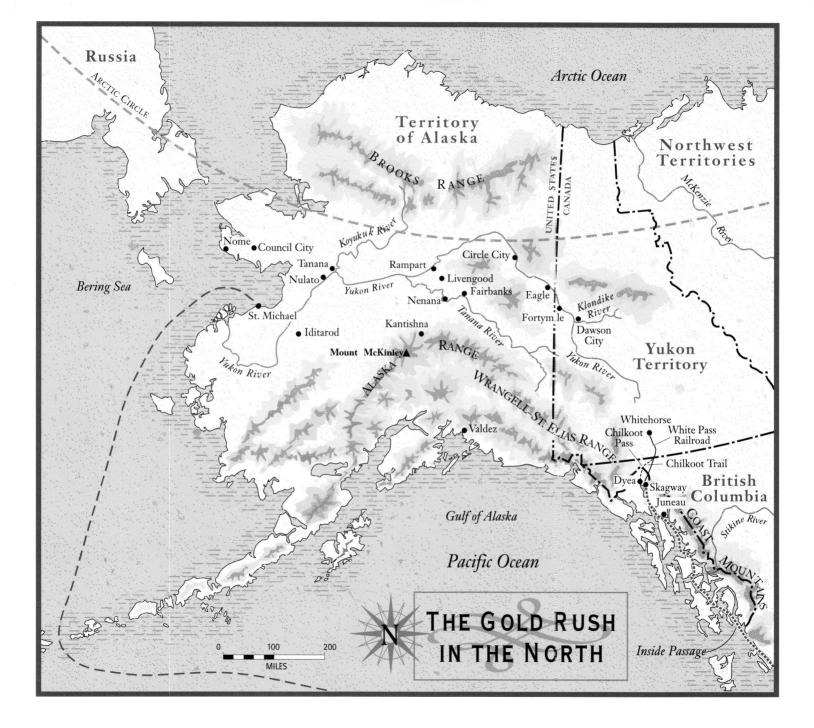

Russia

ARCTIC CIRCLE

Arctic Ocean

Territory
of Alaska

BROOKS   RANGE

Northwest
Territories

McKenzie River

UNITED STATES | CANADA

Bering Sea

Koyukuk River

Nome   • Council City

Tanana   Rampart   Circle City

Nulato   • Livengood

Yukon River   Fairbanks

Nenana   Eagle   Klondike River

St. Michael   Fortym le

Iditarod   Kantishna   Dawson City

Mount McKinley ▲   RANGE

Tanana River

Yukon River

WRANGELL–ST. ELIAS RANGE

Yukon
Territory

Valdez

Whitehorse   White Pass
Chilkoot   Railroad
Pass

Chilkoot Trail

British
Columbia

Dyea
Skagway

Gulf of Alaska

Juneau   COAST

Sitkine River

Pacific Ocean

Inside Passage

MOUNTAINS

0   100   200
MILES

N

THE GOLD RUSH
IN THE NORTH

CHAPTER 1

Crystal Brilliant Snow

TRAVELING TROUBADOUR

Crystal Snow toured the Klondike again as a young woman launching her career as a soprano.

Crystal Brilliant Snow fingered her gold nugget necklace as she stood in front of a pawnshop near the Seattle docks. Her family was poor again, without a penny to their name. It was hard to believe that less than two years ago, in August 1898, they had possessed $80,000. They had walked off the boat in Seattle with a half dozen sheepskin sacks of gold from their claim on Bonanza Creek, one of the richest in the Klondike. Wealthy beyond their wildest dreams, they had stayed at the elegant Stevens Hotel.

Crystal's father, George, was famous. "George Snow can build and own a half dozen theaters now," one Seattle paper reported. He had bought her fancy new clothes of lace, satin, and velvet.

The Snow family had first come North to Juneau, Alaska, in 1888 to entertain the miners. Since then, they had lived in every gold rush town in the North. When they arrived in Juneau, Crystal was only three and her brother, Monte, five. As tiny tots, the two sang for the miners, who showered them with gold nuggets. Perhaps the two

(above) Gold nugget necklace

(left) Crystal and Monte Snow pose with a dog sled at Fortymile for photographer Veazie Wilson in 1894.

A long line of men, and some women and children, made trip after trip packing their ton of goods over the final steep grade of the Chilkoot Trail.

Children of the Gold Rush

Scene on the summit of
Chilkoot Pass Spring of 1898

Goods and supplies are piled helter skelter in the snow at the summit of the Chilkoot Pass in spring, 1898.

Fortymile Area

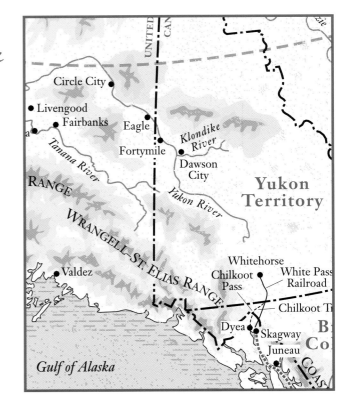

(above) Snow family stage make-up and playbook

(right) The log cabin town of Fortymile, founded in 1886, was home to nearly 1000 people by 1894, including the Snow and Cherosky families.

the treacherous Chilkoot Pass into gold country. They hiked for two weeks through deep snow. Crystal and Monte helped pull a sled with supplies, including a fold-up organ, costumes, and makeup. But Crystal had to leave her favorite doll behind because her father said it was too heavy to carry. During the trip, Crystal and her family were caught in a spring snowstorm. They fired their cookstove and survived for three more days on crackers and tea.

Two days later, safely at the summit, Crystal joyfully looked out over the glaciers and sang one of her favorite songs, "Kathleen Mavoureen."

It may be years and it may be forever,
Oh, why art thou silent, thou voice
of my heart?

When the ice on the Yukon River broke up in June, they floated the 600 miles to Fortymile. About a thousand miners, shopkeepers, and traders lived there in log cabins. Many had Native wives and children. Along with numerous saloons, the town boasted two large log trading posts, a contingent of the Cana-

(above, left) Crystal and Monte Snow performed on stage with their parents in Juneau, Fortymile, and Circle City.

(above, right) Savoy Theatre advertisement

children reminded the lonely men of their families back home. During every performance, Crystal wanted to snatch up the gold nuggets as they fell clattering onto the stage floor. But her mother insisted that they wait until the men had gone home before they collected their riches.

This money helped Crystal's mother, Anna, support the family while her father was out prospecting. Even though her father was a talented actor and singer, he wanted gold most of all. So, in April 1894, the family headed for Fortymile in the Yukon, the first boomtown in the North.

Crystal was only ten when they climbed

dian Mounted Police, and an Anglican church mission on a nearby island. Crystal and Monte attended school at Bishop Bompas's mission with the Athabascan Indian children and learned to speak their language.

But after only a year, Crystal's father insisted that they move again when he heard of a new gold discovery near Circle City, 240 miles down the Yukon River. There they built a two-story log opera house for their performances. When temperatures reached 40 to 50 degrees below zero, too cold for her father and uncle to prospect for gold, the family produced such plays as *Rip Van Winkle*. Mr. Snow played Rip the lazy husband and Mrs. Snow played his nagging wife, while Monte was Rip's son, and Crystal his loyal daughter Menie. They even performed musicals like the *The Mikado* with Crystal and Monte as the two sisters Pitti Sing and Peep Bo. Crystal and Monte attended the new Circle City school, where their teacher was Anna Fulcomer.

AURORA BOREALIS

An Arctic midnight, cold and clear,
The earth enwrapped in purest snow,
The heavens enveloped far and near
In an ethereal, mystic glow
Which ever moving, changing still
A banner made of light it seems;
Guided by an Imperial Will
Across the polar sky it streams.

—Excerpt from unpublished poem by Crystal Snow, Alaska State Library, Juneau, Alaska

In early 1897, news arrived of gold discoveries on the Klondike River. The Snows, along with most of the townspeople, headed up the Yukon River to the new boomtown of Dawson. More than 100,000 people set off on the Klondike Stampede in the winter of 1897–1898, but fewer than half made it.

Dawson soon became the largest town in the North, bustling with energy and enterprise twenty-four hours a day. The Snow family took up mining on Bonanza Creek. And, when they finally struck it rich, Crystal was sure their dreams would come true.

Now, one year later, the money was all gone. Crystal's father had tried to start up a new theatrical company headed for Hawaii. But after dealing with floods, washouts, and broken engagements, and paying the hotel, advertising, and costume expenses, they were broke. Crystal's father decided they should go back to Alaska and try prospecting in Nome, the site of a new gold rush. But they didn't even have enough money left for the trip.

Children of the Gold Rush

LITTLE MARGIE NEWMAN

Little Margie Newman was probably the most popular child performer in Dawson. She arrived with her mother and brother in 1898 when she was only nine. Singing and dancing her way into the hearts of the miners, she reminded them of the children they had left at home, and became a beloved figure, richly rewarded and showered with gold. Known as the "Princess of the Klondike," she played such roles as little Eva in *Uncle Tom's Cabin* and dressed up in a tartan skirt to perform the Scottish ballad "Annie Laurie."

Little Margie Newman (far left) and her brother toured Dawson City on donkeys to promote the opening of their singing act.

So Crystal pawned her gold nugget necklace, her most precious possession, to buy boat tickets for the family. But she insisted that they return to Juneau, the only town she had ever called home. There, the sixteen-year-old Crystal had to enroll as a fifth grader because she had rarely attended a regular school. Five years later she became the second graduate of Juneau High School.

Crystal grew up to become a professional singer and later a teacher. She married a dentist, not a gold miner. She and her husband raised three children in Juneau, and Crystal was proud to say that two of her children graduated from college. Later she served two terms in Alaska's territorial legislature, only the second woman to do so. Throughout her life she wrote about the adventures of her childhood in Alaska and on the Yukon in stories, poetry, plays, and songs.

The Native Packers

"Native women and their young daughters and sons from ten years of age and up were also packing from fifty to seventy-five and one hundred pounds on their backs for miners, earning from ten to twenty dollars per day."

—J. Bernard Moore, *Skagway in Days of Primeval: Diary and Recollection of J. Bernard Moore, 1865–1919.* Lynn Carol Publishing, Skagway: 1977.

(below) These Tlingit children are at Klukwan, the village near present day Haines, Alaska. Their Chilkat tribe controlled trade over what became the Dalton Trail into the Interior.

(above) A Tlingit family at Dyea, the starting point of the Chilkoot Trail. The Chilkoot tribe of the Tlingit people controlled trade into the Yukon River basin before the gold rush. During the rush, many families moved to Dyea to work as packers.

Children of the Gold Rush

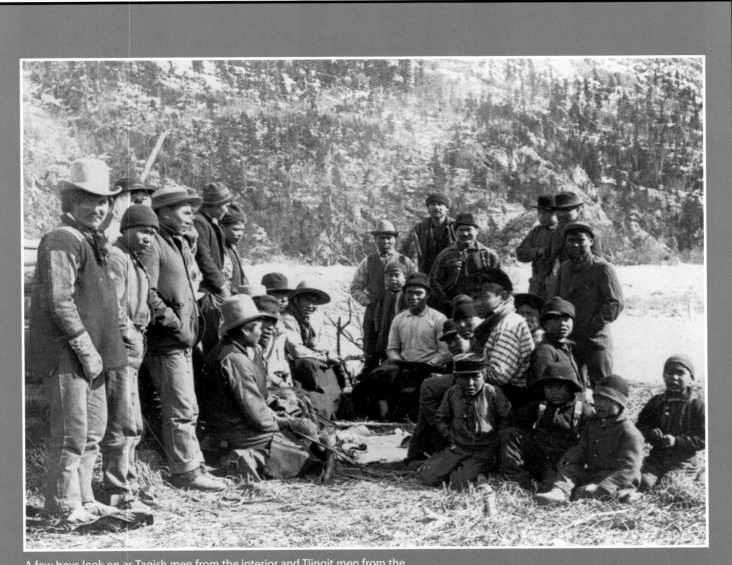

A few boys look on as Tagish men from the interior and Tlingit men from the coast engage in a game of traditional Indian stick gambling. They were between jobs packing supplies for the gold rushers.

CHAPTER II

Axinia &
Helen Cherosky

GOLDEN SISTERS

This portrait of Axinia Cherosky and her sister Helen was probably taken at Circle City in 1899.

"Gold!" whispered Axinia's father. "Your Uncle Pitka and I discovered gold! It must be Lost Preachers' Creek!"

Eleven-year-old Axinia was thrilled. She and her five-year-old sister, Helen, had been waiting several weeks for their father at the trading post at Tanana.

Many times she had listened from her bunk as her father, mother, and uncles talked of the old Russian priest. He had traveled far up the Yukon River many years before and had returned to her grandfather's trading post at Nulato with a small pouch full of gold nuggets. Axinia knew as well as everyone on the Yukon that no one had ever found the lost creek again.

But Axinia could not tell anyone about her father's new discovery. He wanted to keep it a secret, or else the white miners would steal the claims. So, in the fall of 1893, the family boarded a small steam boat and moved about 100 miles up the Yukon River to a place her father knew called Old Portage. There a trail from the river led to the new gold claims. Axinia and Helen were used to moving. Their parents, Sergai and Erinia Cherosky, were descendants of the Russian fur traders and Native Athabascans. For many years they had worked as translators for Jack

McQuesten, the most famous trader on the Yukon, at his trading posts up and down the long and mighty river.

When they arrived at Old Portage, the men cut tall spruce trees and built a cabin. Axinia and Helen gathered piles of soft moss and stuffed it between the logs to chink the cabin against the cold and wind. Soon they had a snug home for the winter.

Still, the cabin was small and lonely. There was no trading post, and no children

Portrait of Erinia Cherosky Callahan, the mother of Axinia and Helen

to play with. The family had brought few food supplies, so the girls and their mother busied themselves with fishing under the ice, drying meat from a moose that Father shot, snaring rabbits, and sewing new fur clothing.

Despite their efforts at secrecy, about a hundred white miners had followed them, hoping to get in on the new find. Early in March, just before the snow melted, the family hiked nearly 60 miles through low swamps to the gold diggings on Birch Creek. When the frozen creek thawed and the water ran down from the hills, the girls watched their father and uncle set up sluice boxes in the middle of the gravelly stream. The men spent all day, week after week, shoveling gravel from the gravel

bars into the sluice boxes to be washed by the creek water.

When it was time for "cleanup," the men stopped the flow through the boxes. Axinia and Helen could see tiny nuggets and flakes of gold in the black sand trapped behind the riffles that were nailed across the bottom of the boxes. Other men were discovering gold on the creeks nearby.

Soon, word came that Jack McQuesten was building a trading post to get supplies to the camp. The new town was called Circle City. With a full moosehide poke of gold, the family walked almost 100 miles to the new post to buy much-needed supplies. In Circle City, Axinia and Helen met up with aunties, uncles, and cousins from downriver, and friends from the

Panorama of Circle City on the banks of the Yukon River

Children of the Gold Rush

other trading posts like the McQuesten children and Crystal and Monte Snow.

Residents of the new town believed education was very important. They raised money to build a school, and the U.S. government sent a teacher, Anna Fulcomer. The new log cabin school opened in October 1896. Axinia and Helen studied with thirty other students. They had no books, so Miss Fulcomer made up lessons every day on the blackboard. The schoolhouse was so cold they had to wear coats inside most of the winter. In the spring, all kinds of bugs emerged from the moss chinking between the logs.

Then, one special day in May, the students heard the cracking and groaning of the river ice. Everyone in town ran to the riverbank to witness the dramatic breakup of the Yukon River. Huge cakes of ice rose up and smashed into each other and onto the shore as the spring meltwater flooded the river. The ice ran downriver for nearly a week, and then it was gone. Soon great steamboats arrived with the first mail and supplies from "Outside" since the fall freeze.

Hundreds of new people arrived to get in on the gold strike. The girls stayed busy helping their mother with her sewing business. But their father Sergai did not profit from this influx of people. The miners had cheated him out of his mining claims. Many miners felt that Natives should not be allowed to own their own claims. Sergai could do nothing about it

Circle City Area

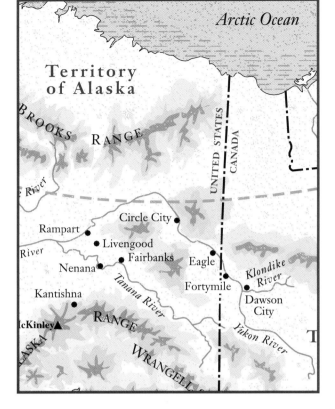

Handmade dress and
beaded velvet toque
made by Erinia Cherosky
Callahan, Helen Callahan
and Axinia Rasmusson

Arctic Ocean

Territory
of Alaska

BROOKS RANGE

River

UNITED STATES | CANADA

Circle City

Rampart
Livengood
Fairbanks
Nenana
Eagle
Kantishna
Fortymile

River

Tanana River

Klondike River

Dawson City

McKinley ▲ RANGE

ALASKA WRANGELL

Yukon River

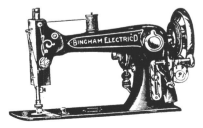

Axinia and Helen (left) pose with their mother Erinia, and new stepfather Dan Callahan (center).

When Helen was eighteen years old, she took a summer trip on a steamer traveling up the Yukon River to Circle City. The following is a quote from her diary:

"July 11, 1911
I stayed up till we got to Forty Mile. I saw the old mission I went to when a little kid, felt a bit lonesome, wished I was a little kid again."

and he became very bitter. Before long, Sergai and Erinia divorced. Sergai returned to his traditional home in the village of Koyukuk, but the girls stayed with their mother in Circle City.

In 1900, at the age of nineteen, Axinia married Nels Rasmusson, a Danish immigrant. They ran a packing business, using a large string of horses to bring supplies to the miners out on the creeks. Nels built a two-story log home and they raised a large family in Circle City.

Thirteen-year-old Helen moved to the new boomtown of Fairbanks after Erinia married packer Dan Callahan. Helen helped her mother start a sewing business there, and proudly finished high school. Later she worked at Alaskan roadhouses and many other jobs. She traveled once to California to visit her Aunt Kate Sonnickson, her mother's sister, who had married a white miner in Fortymile. Helen never married. Her happiest years were spent teaching with missionaries in the village of Fort Yukon, north of Fairbanks.

(right) This prospector scoops water into the top of his gold rocker. His partner is hauling up pay dirt with a windlass.

(below) Klondike advertisement, 1898, shows typical prospector panning for gold.

GOLD PANNING

Gold found in the gravel of streams and rivers is called placer gold. Over many millions of years, gold had washed down from the hills in the Yukon country and settled into the valleys. Early prospectors explored the remote streams with shovel, pick, and gold pan. Into the wide, flat pan they scooped the promising sand and gravel. Then, squatting by the stream, they swirled water over the gravel to wash away the dirt and rocks until only the gold remained.

Children of the Gold Rush

GRAPHIE GRACIE CARMACK: DAUGHTER OF THE DISCOVERY

Graphie Gracie Carmack was only three years old in 1896 when her parents, Kate and George Carmack, and uncles, Skookum Jim and Tagish Charlie, found gold at Rabbit Creek. The richest concentration of gold ever discovered, this find set off the Klondike Stampede.

Kate was a Native Taglish woman. George, a white prospector, had lived with Kate and her relatives for many years, trapping, fishing, hunting, and even packing for money over the Chilkoot Trail.

The discovery at Rabbit Creek, soon renamed Bonanza Creek, changed their lives and the lives of everyone in the Yukon and Alaska. But it did not bring happiness or riches to Graphie. Her father deserted her mother, and both parents fought to keep Graphie. She spent some years with her mother in the Native Yukon settlement of Carcross, and later lived in California with her father and stepmother.

(above) George, Kate, and their daughter, Graphie Gracie, Carmack circa 1898

(left) Kate, Graphie Gracie, and George Carmack in front of their cabin on their discovery claim on Bonanza Creek

CHAPTER III

Ethel Anderson

ROCKING FOR GOLD ON THE CREEKS

Ethel Anderson (center) and her brothers, Dewey and Clay, take a sled ride with their dog, Bruce.

In early September 1898, six-year-old Ethel Anderson stood on the deck of the *SS Utopia* as it made its way north through the rocking waves of the Inside Passage. Beside her, baby brother Clay cried. Her seasick mother was unable to care for him. In addition, the food was awful and they were the only children aboard. Ethel had been thrilled to leave the hard times of Bellingham behind, but nothing was working out as she had hoped.

For seven days they chugged through the rough waters from Seattle to Skagway. They were headed for the Klondike to meet their father. He had left the year before, hoping to strike it rich. "Gold! Gold! Gold!" That's all people on the boat talked about. Would it be that grand? she wondered.

At Skagway, the entire beach was covered with supplies, and people swarmed around in confusion. Ethel's

Ethel Anderson and her fellow students gather with their teacher on Bonanza Creek. Ethel is the blond girl in the black dress.

The community of Grand Forks sprang up at the junction of Bonanza and Eldorado Creeks, the two richest gold creeks in the Klondike. This photo was taken in 1899.

father was still 900 miles away up north in gold country.

The next day, the Anderson family took an open tram car on the brand-new railroad over White Pass Summit. As the tiny train climbed high up into the mountains, Ethel looked down hundreds of feet at the trail below. Just a year earlier, it teemed with horses and prospectors. But the trail had been so grueling that thousands of horses, and even some people, had died. Ethel could still make out some bones. The thought of the dead horses and the feel of the chilly wind in the open car made her cry. Why had she wanted to come to such a place?

At Whitehorse, the family boarded the last riverboat of the season for the 600-

Children of the Gold Rush

mile voyage down the Yukon River to Dawson. Day by day, Ethel watched as more and more ice formed on the river. In turn, the boat moved more and more slowly, trying to make its way through the thickening chunks. Finally, the ice locked the boat in the middle of the river. Ethel and the rest of the passengers had to walk the last few miles to Dawson.

When they reached Dawson, there was Father, waiting on shore. After big hugs all around, he loaded them onto a sled pulled by a big horse named Star. "Home, Star! Take my family home!" he yelled. "Home" was a 14-by-20-foot log cabin 20 miles from Dawson on Eldorado Creek. It had one window and a floor made of split tree poles that were hard to walk on. But Ethel didn't care. She was happy to be with her father again. She slept soundly in her bed, a bunk built into the wall and covered with spruce boughs.

Ethel's father had tried to prospect for gold, but instead he found he could make more money cutting down trees in the nearby forest. The miners paid him well for lumber to use for firewood, mining shafts, and sluice boxes.

Even though their father was not a miner, Ethel and her brothers tried their hands at gold mining. They dragged buckets full of gravel from the creek near the cabin. Then, with dippers full of water, they washed it away in their own little rocker until only the gold remained. Some days, they found $14 worth of gold—twice what their father had made every week back home in Bellingham.

Ethel also helped her mother bake cinnamon rolls and brown bread to sell to the hungry miners. The miners paid them a dollar a loaf—a huge sum at that time.

Ethel and her two brothers loved to play outdoors at the creek, but Mother warned them to stay away from the machinery and open mining shafts. Inside, they played with the dolls that family friends had sent for Christmas. However, they arrived six months late, on the first riverboat in May.

Diseases like smallpox, typhoid fever, and measles spread throughout the camp. But Ethel's mother used a home remedy to prevent her children from getting sick. Two or three times a day, she sprinkled yellow sulfur powder over the top of the hot stove. The children stood close to the stove and watched the pretty yellow, red, and purple colors swirling above. They did not even realize they were breathing in germ-killing fumes to keep them healthy. Although some people died during the epidemic, the Anderson children never became ill.

In the spring, Ethel helped her mother plant lettuce, radish, and onion seeds on

"Food was scarce that first winter … No one could foresee the thousands of sourdoughs who would invade the Klondike land, many of whom were out of grub. But our papa was a good hunter and Bonanza Creek was a rabbit heaven. Mother cleaned rabbits, rabbits, rabbits . . . . . Mother never ate rabbit after we left the Klondike.

—Ethel Anderson Becker, "Little Girl in the Klondike Goldfields," *Alaskan Sportsman,* November 1962

Klondike Area

Typical items of everyday use include a hotel advertisement, enamel serving tray, and playing cards

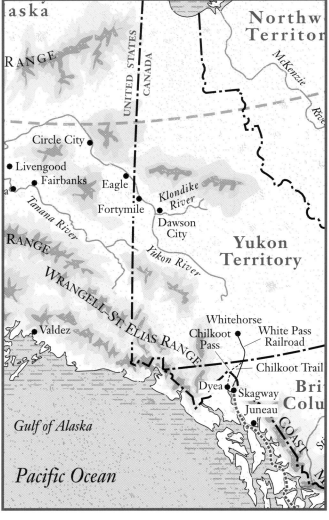

the sod-covered cabin roof. The heat from the cabin helped the delicious vegetables grow quickly. After a long winter of beans, dried potatoes, and canned food, the family enjoyed the fresh food.

In the summer, Miss Lind arrived on Eldorado Creek and started a school in a tent. Ethel and Dewey loved the reading and math lessons and never missed a day.

In 1902, when Ethel was seven, the Andersons returned to Bellingham. People stared at her gold nugget jewelry. She was startled to live in a neighborhood with roads and streetcars. Their big frame house had electric lights and even a telephone— things unheard of on Eldorado Creek.

Although Ethel never lived in the North again, she could not forget her gold rush days. When she grew up, Ethel collected thousands of gold rush photographs and published them in magazine articles and books she wrote about the Klondike.

NO. ABOVE ON OPHIR.
GEO. BUNKER OPERATOR

STAKING A CLAIM

Where gold was found, a "discovery claim" could be staked. Subsequent claims were laid out up- and downstream, and numbered as "1 above" or "1 below" the discovery claim. Early miners used new tools such as the gold rocker, which sorted, sifted, and washed the gold out of the gravel while the miner rocked the box with the handle.

With enough lumber, a long sluice box could be set up in the stream. Workers shoveled the gravel into the box and channeled the stream water over it, washing the gravel away. Gold was caught in the riffles on the bottom of the box.

Sluicing on Ophir Creek

Children of the Gold Rush

Skagway

(above) Children gather to watch a pack train on the main street in Skagway prepare to head up the White Pass to the Klondike in 1898.

(below) Skagway newsboys pose with their papers in 1898. The man on the far right is playing with a bear cub.

Ben Moore's young captive moose is being trained to harness by Ben's sister Edith.

Children of the Gold Rush

MOORE FAMILY OF SKAGWAY

Bennie, Edith, and Frances Moore were among the first children to live in Skagway. The family owned the biggest house in town and rode in a small carriage pulled by a tame moose.

Their father, Ben, and grandfather, Captain Moore, had started a trading post there in 1887, ten years before the Klondike gold rush. Their mother, Minnie, was a Tlingit Indian from Kluckwan whom their father had met at a potlatch. When the town of Skagway sprang up, the Moores' original cabin ended up in the middle of the street. By that time, however, the family was wealthy from trading, selling land, and building docks.

Even though they were rich, these mixed-race children and their mother had a difficult time because many townspeople were prejudiced against Native people. But that did not prevent all the children in town from attending Bennie's ninth birthday party, dressed in their finest clothes. The party was held in August 1900, just days before Bennie and Edith left for boarding school in Tacoma. Bennie and Edith returned to Skagway on their summer vacations.

In 1906 the family moved to Victoria, British Columbia, and Minnie and Ben later divorced. Young Ben grew up to become a cameraman in Hollywood and tried for years to have his family's story made into a movie. The Moore children, grand-children, and great-grandchildren grew up with little knowledge about their Tlingit relatives, though they all knew about Captain Moore, the founder of Skagway. Not until this generation did they realize their Native roots.

Mrs. Moore and her children, Ben, Edith, and baby Frances.

CHAPTER IV

Robert Farnsworth

ARMY POST ON THE YUKON

Robert Farnsworth and friends
on the steamer Humbolt, bound
for Seattle, after leaving Alaska,
August 1901

On December 31, 1899, an ice storm filled the air with millions of crystals. Northern lights danced in the sky overhead. It was 70 degrees below zero in Tanana, Alaska, but eleven-year-old Robert Farnsworth stood outside to admire the sight. He wore a full suit of fur clothing made by the local Native women to keep him warm. Later, he would write about that night: "The aurora borealis hung in the skies like washing on a line, waving around."

Robert had mushed his own dog team and made friends with an Athabascan chief named Chief Joseph. Sometimes he and his father went caribou hunting on snowshoes with the Native people. Once, they found a herd of more than a thousand caribou and shot thirty-six of them. There was enough meat to feed the whole town and the post throughout the winter.

Robert's arrival in Alaska six months earlier already seemed like a distant memory. A scared ten-year-old, he had come north by ship with his stepmother and father. His natural mother had died when he was a baby. His father was the lieutenant commander of Army Company E, which had just been assigned to Alaska. Because of the Klondike gold rush, the

Robert feeding his dogs on the Army post Fort Egbert, at Eagle

North had become a wild place with lots of claim-jumping, robberies, and even murders. The U.S. Army hoped that a military post on the Yukon River would help maintain order.

When they arrived in St. Michael, Alaska, in July 1899, it was elelven o'clock at night. But the sun was still high in the sky, so Robert refused to go to bed. His parents tried to tell him about the midnight sun and how it did not set during the summer. But Robert would not listen. He stayed up all night just like the Inupiaq Eskimo children he met there who played at night and slept during the day.

Soon the family and the soldiers traveled up to the village of Tanana where the Tanana River joins the Yukon. There the soldiers constructed Fort Gibbon.

Robert was the only child at the fort. Because there was no school there, his mother taught him lessons.

After the long winter, the first boat to come upriver in May brought fresh fruit and mail. Sadly, Robert learned that his grandfather had died in January. But fortunately, another family, including several children, arrived on the boat. Robert threw his arms around the oldest boy, who instantly gave him a black eye. The family had brought along the first "funny paper" he had ever seen. Robert recovered his pride by reading the "Katzen-jammer Kids" over and over, laughing and crying at their antics.

Orders also arrived from Washington. The Farnsworths and Company E were transferred to Fort Egbert at Eagle,

A panoramic view of Eagle City in 1900

Children of the Gold Rush

Alaska, 800 miles up the Yukon River. Eagle was a small settlement, not far from the Canadian border and only 120 miles from the boomtown of Dawson. But Robert never managed to visit Dawson because his mother considered it too wild for a young boy.

With its barracks for 102 enlisted men, a gymnasium, baseball fields, a library of 1,200 books, and a large stable for horses and mules, Fort Egbert was much larger than Fort Gibbon. Robert enjoyed his new home and many new activities.

One of his father's responsibilities was to supervise the construction of a telegraph line to connect Eagle with the rest of the world. Then there would be no more waiting for news from outside. In addition, Robert and some of the townspeople helped

his father collect specimens of birds and bears for the Smithsonian Institution in Washington, D.C. Years later, Robert would proudly see them on display there.

When ice breakup came in June, Farnsworth was reassigned to Fort Vancouver, Washington. The family sadly left Fort Egbert. Robert had grown out of all his clothing, so his mother cut him a pair of pants out of an old yellow army blanket. He also wore a pair of his mother's old shoes with the heels cut off and an old, shabby coat. When the family reached Seattle, they were such an awful sight that the taxicab driver refused to take them unless they paid in advance.

Robert never again lived in Alaska, but his father and mother returned for another tour of duty in 1910. After his father died,

Tanana Area

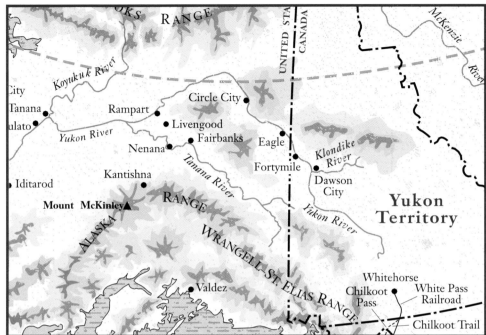

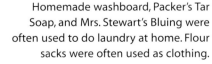
Homemade washboard, Packer's Tar Soap, and Mrs. Stewart's Bluing were often used to do laundry at home. Flour sacks were often used as clothing.

Robert Farnsworth and his mother pose with the troops outside a cabin at Fort Gibbon, the first army post on the Yukon River, near the present village of Tanana.

Robert donated his father's Alaskan papers and photographs to the University of Alaska Fairbanks' archives. Later he wrote a manuscript about his adventures in the North country and the interesting people he had met.

"On the boat North there was trouble with the provisions. The crackers had bugs and maggots in them and the oatmeal had large white worms. When cooked they swelled up and I can remember picking them out and lining them up alongside my plate. My mother put a stop to this."

—Robert Farnsworth, "An Army Brat Goes to Alaska," *Alaska Journal,* (two parts) vol #3, Summer 1977; vol. #4, Autumn 1977

Cliff. Utawaat - Mike - Hatch - Izguierdo. Derech

Children of the Gold Rush

(*above*) Robert visited, hunted, and trapped with this Athabascan band who lived near Eagle.

(*opposite, top left*) Robert learned to enjoy the outdoor life, even in mid-winter. Here he is on snowshoes with his mother and father.

(*opposite, top right*) Clifford Hancock, a former Pullman porter, quit his railroad job to go to Alaska as the Farnsworth's servant.

(*opposite, below*) Robert poses with his own dog team: Cliff, Utawaat, Mike, Hatch, Esquierdo, and Deracho. *Esquierdo* and *deracho* are the Spanish words for "left" and "right." The dogs might have been named by Clifford, who spoke fluent Spanish.

CHAPTER V

Antoinette & Annette Mayo

TRADING POST TWINS

Margaret and Al Mayo and family, around 1905. This picture was taken just as Thirteen-year-old Kitty, on the left, is getting ready to go to boarding school in San Francisco. Twins Antoinette and Annette are on the right.

Anto and Nettie hid behind the fancy pillows on the couch in the corner, watching the beautiful ladies in elegant dresses. The twins were only five, but they would always remember the winter of 1898-1899, when the great riverboats were trapped in the ice of the Yukon River. Thousands of Klondike gold-seekers from all over the world were stranded in the town of Rampart.

The newcomers spent the winter in the newly built restaurants and saloons, gambling and drinking. Among the stampeders were Wyatt Earp and his beautiful wife, Josie, who was a frequent visitor at the Mayo home. The twins watched as their mother, Margaret, made Josie Earp a beautiful white fur parka.

The twins were born in 1894, the next to youngest in a large family of twelve children. Their mother was the daughter of an Athabascan Indian chief in Nuke-lekayet, an important trading site where the Tanana and Yukon Rivers meet. Every year, Koyukon, Gwichin, Tanana, and Ingalik Athabascan Indians came to Nuke-lekayet from up and down the rivers for a great trading festival. Some of the Inupiaq Eskimos from far up north even attended. The twins' father, Al "Cap" Mayo, was a former circus acrobat with a lively sense of humor. He had lived in the

The town of Rampart was founded in 1896 and had two large log trading posts as well as cabins, restaurants, hotels, and saloons.

(right) Anto and Nettie and their sister Florence, (1, 2, and 3) and their classmates pose in front of their school.

(below) The first government school in Rampart in 1907

Yukon for more than twenty years and was one of the best known American traders.

Anto and Nettie lived in the big log trading post in Rampart. Their father and older brothers had built it three years earlier, after gold was discovered in nearby creeks. Father spent almost every day behind the big counter in the trading post. The twins joined him there and they had plenty to see and do as they played. Shiny fox and marten furs hung in bundles from the ceiling. Stacks of round, flat beaver pelts were piled everywhere. Behind the

Children of the Gold Rush

counter were rows of canned foods and stacks of fifty-pound sacks of flour, sugar, and beans. On the shelves were bolts of bright calico cloth. And in the corners were the picks, shovels, axes, saws, and shiny round gold pans—the tools of the prospector's trade.

The miners paid for their goods from their heavy pokes filled with gold dust and nuggets. Father weighed out the gold on the big gold scale on the counter. Anto and Nettie liked to dig the dirt and dust out of the cracks in the floor. Then they

panned it to recover the gold that had spilled from the miners' pokes.

In the winter the girls went outside every day, even when temperatures dipped to 50 degrees below zero. They strapped on their snowshoes and followed the wild animal trails outside of town. There they helped their mother and aunties set snares for rabbits. Mother sewed them warm mittens, mukluks, and parkas out of rabbit, moose, and caribou skins, so they were never cold. The girls loved to watch their mother do fancy beadwork on the moose-

Rampart Area

Athabascan moosehide
beaded hunter's bag

Territory of Alaska

BROOKS RANGE

UNITED STATES | CANADA

Nome Council City

Koyukuk River

Tanana Rampart Circle City

Nulato Livengood

Yukon River Fairbanks Eagle

Nenana Fortymile

St. Michael

Iditarod Kantishna

Mount McKinley▲ ALASKA RANGE

Yukon River WRANGELL-ST. ELIAS

Tanana River

Yuk

Valdez

The *Governor Pingree* was built in the fall of 1898 at St. Michael for a group of gold seekers trying to reach the Klondike. All of the passengers were stuck in Rampart for the winter after the boat got stuck in the ice on the Yukon.

(above) Decorated Athabascan chief's jacket signifies wealth and position.

(right) Beaded moosehide pillow cover made by Margaret Mayo

hide. She made and decorated moccasins, parkas, and vests for the family, and beautiful pillows to sell. And she always gave the twins a small piece to practice on.

In the summer, the girls helped their mother and the other women set nets in the Yukon River to catch salmon. Afterwards, they cut up the fish and hung it on racks to dry so they would have food for the winter. They kept a slow fire burning underneath to make delicious smoked fish.

Mother was also the town midwife. Often the twins would hear a knock on the door late at night. Then their mother would leave the house to help deliver a new baby or heal a sick person.

In 1910 the U.S. government built a school in Rampart. Now Anto and Nettie would not have to leave their parents to attend a boarding school "Outside" as their older brothers and sisters had. They could go to high school in their own town.

Anto and Nettie grew up to raise families of their own. From a small settlement in the wilderness, Rampart had become a thriving town during the gold rush. The twins and their Athabascan people adapted to the new civilization brought by the gold rush, with its schools, stores, riverboats, and government. Today their grandchildren and great-grandchildren live in Fairbanks and interior Alaska.

Children of the Gold Rush

TRADING POSTS

The Native Athabascans had lived off the land, hunting and fishing, for thousands of years. When the British, Russian, and American traders came, they trapped furs to trade for flour, sugar, tea, cloth, and beads. To trade for a gun, they made a pile of beaver skins as high as the gun.

When the white miners arrived, they didn't know how to live off the land. So the miners depended on the food and supplies that the traders brought upriver by steamboat and sold at the trading posts.

All kinds of goods were for sale inside the big North American Trading and Transportation Company store at Rampart.

CHAPTER VI

Klondy Nelson

LIFE WITHOUT PAPA

Klondy Nelson at age five with her mother Alma, when they arrived in Nome in 1902

When Klondy Nelson was born in 1897, her father insisted on naming her after the Klondike, the newest gold strike in the North. Two weeks later, he left South Dakota for that very gold rush. Klondy and her mama had not seen him since. Klondy's mama had come over from Sweden only the year before and could barely speak English.

When Klondy was five years old, she and her mama traveled thousands of miles to join her papa in Alaska. The Arctic air was chilly when they arrived in Nome in October 1902 on the the last boat of the season. Hundreds of people were milling around on the beach, gathering their supplies or panning for gold. But not her papa. He was at his claim 60 miles away in Ophir Creek, and had sent his partner, Blueberry Pete, to meet them.

After a long trip by horse-drawn coach and dogsled, Klondy finally found Papa. He was a big dark man in a long fur coat standing in front of a tiny cabin buried under the snow. Their new home was just big enough for a double bunk for her

The local Inupiaq Eskimos taught Klondy to fish through the ice.

Council City, where Klondy first took violin lessons, was just a small settlement on the Niukluk River.

parents, a small bunk for Klondy, a wood-stove, a tiny table, one chair, and a few shelves made of packing crates. The entire place was smaller than her bedroom back in Blacktail Gulch.

Even though she had no playmates, Klondy discovered many things to do in Ophir Creek. She watched the reindeer herders in the nearby hills. She helped her mother make caribou and rabbit stew. She played with the new rag doll her mama had made out of one of Papa's old socks. But she longed to spend time with her papa, who worked long hours on his mining claim. Many nights he did not get home until Klondy was already asleep.

When December came, the temperature fell to 50 degrees below zero. It was too cold to play outside, even with the warmest fur parka. Plus, it was dark almost all the time, with only a few hours of dim twilight around noon. So Klondy and her mama spent their time indoors, planning a traditional Swedish Christmas. They made cranberry and popcorn chains and Swedish cookies for the Christmas tree at the miners' bunkhouse. On Christmas Eve, when Klondy entered the bunkhouse in

Children of the Gold Rush

Klondy and her family, including brother Ophir, stand on the porch of their beautiful white log cabin in Nome during a period of prosperity.

her pretty red dress and her hair in ringlets, some of the miners began to cry. Missing their own children far away, they showered her with presents of gold nuggets. Her papa made her a tiny dollhouse from a syrup tin.

After a long winter of work, Klondy's papa found little gold in his sluice box. So the next winter the family moved to the nearby town of Council, where they bought a store and her papa quit prospecting—for a while. Klondy had other children to play with, a school to attend, and a new baby brother named Ophir. Although Council was just a small mining settlement, a German professor lived there who gave Klondy violin lessons.

But Klondy's papa was not a successful shopkeeper and took up prospecting once again. He set out for Nome with Blueberry Pete and staked the Solo Mine on the newly discovered Third Beach. There he finally struck it rich and bought the family a beautiful white house in Nome. Just when things seemed to be looking up for Klondy and her family, her papa invested all the money in more mining equipment and set off looking for gold

Nome Area

ARCTIC CIRCLE

BRO

Koyukuk River

Nome

Council City

Tanana

Nulato

Yukon River

Bering Sea

St. Michael

Iditarod

Mount McKin

Yukon River

ALASKA

K

W. A. BANK

Black sand and gold from the bottom of the gold pan was transfered to the blower pan. After miners blew the sand away from the gold, the gold was stored in a moosehide poke.

Mrs. Staple's class, Nome

THE SCHOOLHOUSE

"There was no schoolhouse in Council, because there were only seven pupils, so we held classes in the Presbyterian Church. Our teacher was a Mrs. Horning, who wore her hair in a pompadour, and a shirtwaist with a high collar. She looked exactly like a Gibson girl. She stood where the pulpit was, and we sat in front of her in the slanting pews. I was the only one in the first grade, and my feet didn't even reach the floor.

"I hadn't been with other children before, so at first I was very shy and serious. My seat was near the window, and I could dig my fingernails down through the heavy frost or suck my finger until it got warm and draw funny pictures on the pane. The other children watched me and began to titter. We all wore long underwear and wool stockings, bloomers, and sweaters, and when the big pot-bellied stove warmed the church, it was a heavenly sensation to scratch."

—**Klondy Nelson,** *Daughter of the Gold Rush,*
with Corey Ford, Random House, New York, 1958

The Fourth of July was a big celebration at every gold camp. Here, boys participate in a race at the celebration in Nome.

Children of the Gold Rush

farther north. Klondy's mama took in boarders to support the children.

Klondy had planned to go to Seattle to study the violin after high school graduation. But since her father had taken all their money, Blueberry Pete helped organize a benefit concert to pay for her trip. Following Mama's death a few years later, once again Blueberry Pete found money for Ophir to join her in Seattle.

After her studies, Klondy worked as a musician. Hurt by her papa's neglect, she swore she would never return to Alaska. But that was before she fell in love and married wildlife biologist Frank Dufresne, a man she had met while mushing dogs in Nome. They moved to Fairbanks, and Frank became Alaska's first fish and game warden. Klondy and their children traveled with him as he worked around the huge state. Years later, on one of these trips, Klondy ran into her papa far up on the Yukon, still prospecting, still crazed for gold.

$30,000 worth of gold from Captain E. W. Johnston's claim at No. 8 Cooper Gulch near Nome, August 18, 1907

Klondy never had a father she could depend on. She had to make her own dreams come true. But even though her childhood was difficult, she worked hard to make a happy life with her husband and children. When her children were grown, Klondy wrote a book about her Alaskan childhood.

(above) Nearly 30,000 people landed at Nome in 1900, and most ended up camped on the beach. Their white tents lined the shore for more than ten miles.

(left) At Nome gold could be mined right on the beaches. A claim was a shovel's width on either side of the sluice box.

Nome

(right) Front Street in Nome in July 1900 was a crowded scene of disorder, with thousands hoping to make their fortune.

(below) Wood framed buildings lined the narrow Front Street in Nome in winter 1907.

The Niukluk River valley on the Seward Peninsula, some 60 miles east of Nome, was the center of the Council City mining district—the second richest district on the peninsula. The trees in this valley are some of the few that grow on the tundra-covered Seward Peninsula.

Children of the Gold Rush

MINING UNDERGROUND ON №3 A FAIRBANKS CREEK

MINING UNDERGROUND

In the North the gold in ancient streambeds is sometimes buried under tens or even hundreds of feet of permanently frozen dirt called "overburden" or muck. Prospectors had to dig deep shafts down to the gravel to find the gold. They lit fires every night, and in the morning dug down through the few feet of thawed dirt. Then they repeated the process. When they reached the gravel, they hauled it up and panned it in a washtub. Most often, the greatest concentration of gold was on top of the bedrock.

(above) Miners tunneled underground at the bottom of deep mining shafts to reach the ancient buried gravels containing gold.

CHAPTER VII

Cleora Casady

GOLD CAMP CHILDHOOD

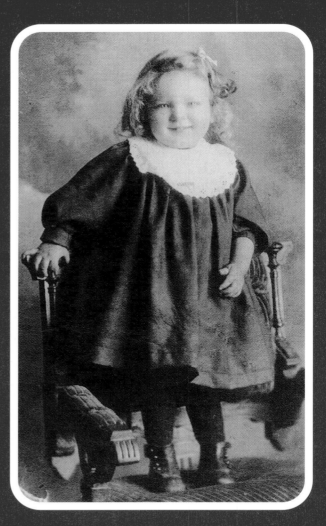

Cleora Casady as a toddler

Six-year-old Cleora Casady woke up early one September morning in 1907 to the sound of barking dogs. Outside the tiny one-room cabin in Fairbanks it was snowing, the first snowfall of the year. Her stepfather was packing the sled and hitching up the dogs. He was going prospecting and would be away the whole winter. Although Cleora knew she might miss him later, secretly she was relieved to see him go. Too many nights she had hid under the bed when he came home drunk and argued with her mother.

Only the year before, Cleora had arrived in Fairbanks by boat with her mother and stepbrother, Adolph, to join her stepfather. But things had not gone well from the start. Like many prospectors, her father had not found the gold he was looking for and spent too much time drinking at the saloon.

With her father gone, life was calmer but not much easier. Adolph and Cleora attended school, but Cleora's mother had to work so the family would have food to eat. She sewed for a woman's dress shop and nursed the sick all through the long winter. In the summer, Cleora and her mother hiked up into the hills a few miles outside of town to pick blueberries. Every day they gathered about thirty pounds, and Adolph and Cleora sold them door-to-door for twenty-five cents a pound. Cleora's mother was ashamed and did not want anyone to know how poor they were. She had to make the children's underwear out of flour sacks. She made sure that Cleora and Adolph were always neat and clean. Cleora's clothes might not be new, but they were always washed and pressed, and her hair done up in ringlets.

After Mr. Casady returned from prospecting, Cleora's mother divorced him. He moved back to Oregon, taking Adolph with him. Cleora missed her brother a great deal and thought about him for the rest of her life.

Cleora Casady with her mother and stepbrother Adolph

Riverboats brought goods and people to the bustling Fairbanks waterfront in 1906.

Children of the Gold Rush

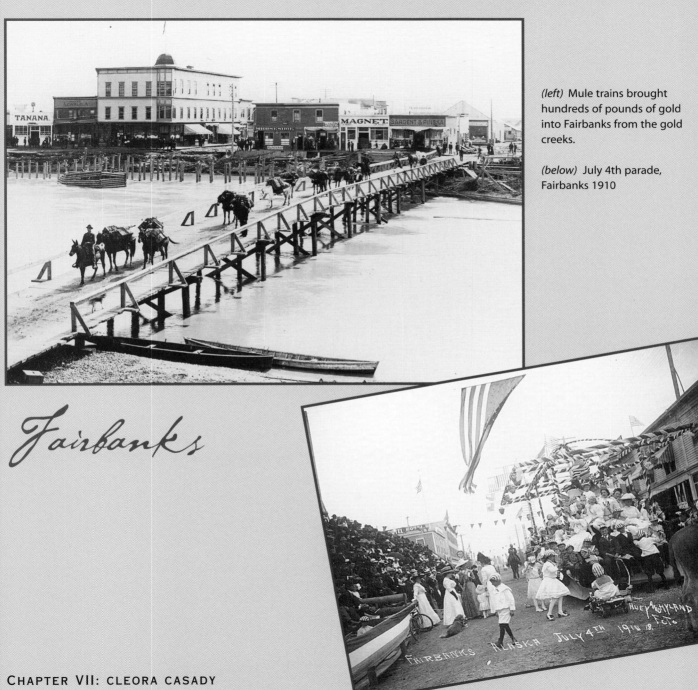

(left) Mule trains brought hundreds of pounds of gold into Fairbanks from the gold creeks.

(below) July 4th parade, Fairbanks 1910

Fairbanks

Fairbanks Area

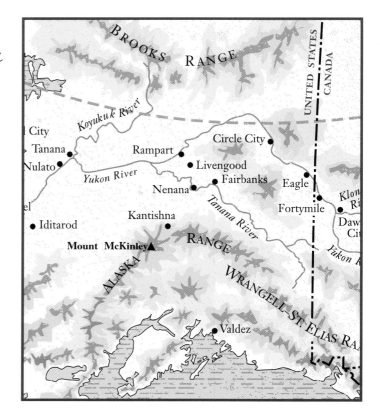

(left) Victorian doll belonging to Emily Romig, the daughter of missionaries who lived in Bethel for many years.

(below) Goods and supplies were tied onto wooden pack saddles and loaded onto horses, donkeys, and mules.

Cleora's mother took a job as a waitress in the mess hall of a large mining operation on Engineer Creek, 10 miles from Fairbanks. She and Cleora moved into a tiny room at the back of the mine owner's house. Cleora could not go to school because it was too far from town. The mine owner's wife strictly instructed her to stay in her room and not be a bother in the main house.

So Cleora spent most of the long winter days by herself, playing with paper dolls and looking at magazines. Standing on a milk crate, she used her fingernails to scrape a peephole in the frosty windowpane. Through it she watched teams of horses pass by, hauling huge loads of birch and spruce wood to the boiler house. Every night at six o'clock, once the miners had left the mess hall, Cleora ran over to have dinner with her mother and the Japanese cooks. It was her favorite time of day.

Cleora did not look forward to Christmas that year. There would be no new dress sewn by her mother, no school Christmas program, and no Adolph to share the excitement. But luckily, at the last minute, Cleora and her mother were invited to the mine owner's Christmas Eve party. When she opened the door, Cleora entered a magical world filled with candles, decorations, and a beautiful Christmas tree. Under the tree sat a lovely doll

Cleora as a young woman in a mining camp

Cleora's Diary October 30, 1912:

"Hitched prince up and went to Ester all by my lonesome. prince went perty good but came home twice as fast. I thought I frose my feet but I did not."

—Cleora, eleven years old, with permission from Donna Rankin

with real eyelashes and long curls, a lacy pink dress, and white shoes. Cleora was stunned when the mine owner's wife placed the doll in her arms. With her doll Annabelle by her side, the rest of the winter seemed a little less lonely.

The following summer, the mine closed and Cleora and her mother moved to yet another mining camp. At St. Patrick's Creek, nine-year-old Cleora ran a dog team with her own small sled. Sometimes she even earned money by collecting

When the new discoveries were made at Livengood in 1914, the scene was not much different from mining camps twenty-five years before. Both Vide and Cleora went on the gold rush to Livengood with their families.

"I spent my 14th birthday, September 21, 1915, cooking over a campfire and sleeping in a tent on the bank of the Tolavana River. Unfortunately the small river boat I was traveling on had sprung a leak and sunk on the gold rush to Livengood. Mother and I were going to join my new stepfather who had staked a claim on Mike Hess Creek, a fifteen mile hike from the boat landing, and about 125 miles from Fairbanks. For me it would be another winter far from school."

—from Cleora's unpublished autobiography, University of Alaska Fairbanks, Archives, Alaska and Polar Regions Department, Jo Anne Wold Collection

Children of the Gold Rush

(left, top) The Tanana Valley Railroad was constructed in 1905–1906. Its 30 miles of track led from Fairbanks to the gold creeks. Miners and their families lived in small towns on every creek.

(left, below) This claim at 10 Below Cleary Creek was the richest on the creek and belonged to Vide's father O. P. Gaustad.

Garden Island School in Fairbanks, around 1906. Cleora is in the bottom row, third from left. Adolph is in the middle row, third from right.

the mail at Ester gold camp, which was 4 miles away. When the dogs dumped her off the sled, she picked herself up and got back on, just as Adolph had taught her.

Cleora missed another year of school that year, but she loved to read and studied whatever books and magazines she could find. She also learned about gold mining. "I pestered the men with questions, and hoped someday I might strike it rich," she would later write.

When Cleora turned fourteen, her mother remarried and they spent the winter at the new gold rush camp of Livengood, 80 miles north of Fairbanks. Cleora earned money by baking bread for the workers at her new stepfather's mine. In Livengood she met her first boyfriend, a miner named George Bachner. Even though she had sworn she would never marry a miner, three years later, when she was seventeen, they tied the knot.

Cleora raised her children in the gold camps until they were old enough to attend school. Then she insisted that they move to Fairbanks so they could receive the education she had missed. Cleora worked hard to make a happy life with her husband and children. Their house was full of activity and she was never again lonely, as she had been as a child. But the loss of Adolph was a lifelong sorrow for her. At the age of sixteen, he had run away from his father and died a few years later at a lumber camp in Oregon.

Cleora became a famous pioneer who told stories about the old days to the young people of Fairbanks. When her first husband died, she married another prospector, Arne Erickson.

On January 7, 1915, Cleora wrote the following poem in her poetry book:

Children of the Gold Rush

I live in Fairbanks, Alaska
Am thirteen years old
We came here in nineteen-seven
To find some gold.

Most people think
This land is of ice and snow.
But if they were here,
They wouldn't think so.

We "kids" have a skating rink,
The boys shovel away the snow.
And when we have nothing to do,
It's dog riding we go.

We've lived on the creek,
All of one winter we cooked,
For men who looked for gold
They never found it, so out they sold.

Gold is scarce,
No matter where you look
But once in a while, people find it
They are mostly crooks.

If a deserving man makes a stake,
Some crook claims it.
And then the lawyers,
more than their share take.

Inside pages and cover of Cleora's diary,
age thirteen

VIDE GAUSTAD BARTLETT

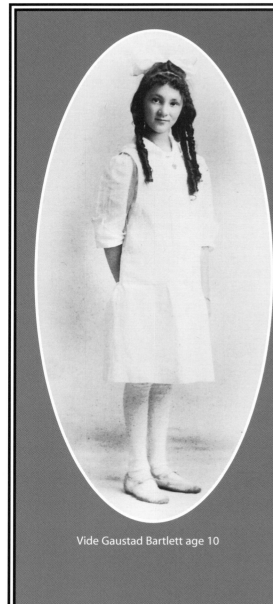

Vide Gaustad Bartlett age 10

Vide Gaustad lived in many of the same gold camps as Cleora Casady. But while Cleora was poor, Vide was wealthy. Her father had the richest claim on Cleary Creek. Vide was much better dressed—and more warmly, too. "Mother made most of my clothing—long underwear, heavy stockings, and felt boots, heavy dresses and coats made out of blankets lined with rabbit fur, gloves, and hats."

In 1910, Vide's father sold the Cleary Creek claim, used the money to buy an orange grove near Los Angeles, and the family moved to California.

Vide's mother and father fought a great deal, so in the summer of 1911, Vide and her mother moved back to Fairbanks. Down the street from their new home lived the Bartlett family. Young Bob Bartlett and Vide walked together to the big wooden schoolhouse at Eighth and Cushman. They watched movies and went sledding. Once a week, they joined the crowd to meet the horse-drawn mail stage when it arrived over the trail from Valdez with mail and supplies.

Vide's father soon returned to Alaska to run for political office. He was elected and served in the territorial senate. Then, in 1916, he joined the rush to Livengood. Vide and her mother spent summers in the new gold camp.

When Vide's parents divorced, she and her mother moved back to Los Angeles. Vide graduated from Hollywood High School in California in May 1922. She earned her college degree at UCLA and became a teacher.

Bob Bartlett had been in love with Vide since childhood. He had even proposed to her many times. But Vide did not agree to marry her childhood sweetheart until 1930, when she was 30 years old. Like her father, Bob Bartlett was interested in politics. He became one of Alaska's first two U.S. senators after Alaska achieved statehood in 1959. Vide supported his political career while she raised their children. She continued her civic activities long after his death.

Both Vide and Cleora led long and interesting lives and witnessed Alaska's emergence from a golden territory to the forty-ninth state in the Union.

Children of the Gold Rush

THE CLEAN UP FRED SLEGAR'S GOLD MINE GOLD STREAM CO. FAIRBANKS, ALASKA

Women, children, and miners gather at the sluice box for the cleanup at a mine on Goldstream Creek, near Fairbanks.

DRIFT MINING

If a prospector found gold after digging down to bedrock, the claim might be developed into a mine. At the bottom of the shaft, underground workers dug tunnels, or drifts, following the gold deposits along the ancient streambed. Steam engines operated self-dumping buckets to pull the dirt and gravel out of the ground and pour it onto huge piles. The piles, called "dumps," grew all winter.

In the spring, when running water was again available, the gravel in the dumps was washed through sluice boxes. "Cleanup" was the most exciting time: the operation was stopped, and the miner found out how much gold was in the box.

CHAPTER VIII

IDITAROD
ENTREPRENEUR

Alice McDonald and her son
Donald at Dawson City

Late into the night, eight-year-old Donald McDonald lay on his bunk and listened to the hubbub of the new boomtown. It was August 1910 in Iditarod, Alaska, and the hammering could be heard around the clock under the midnight sun. Donald, his four-year-old sister, Sigrid, and his mother, Alice, lived on Main Street in a big canvas tent on the boardwalk, which their mother operated as a hotel.

For two months, Donald and his family had traveled by steamboat from Fairbanks down the Tanana River to the great Yukon, and finally to the shallow waters of the Innoko River. At first, Sigrid and Donald had wobbly legs because they had been on the boat so long. But they soon adjusted to their new life on dry land.

Both children had been born in gold country—Donald in Dawson and Sigrid in Fairbanks. Their parents had already lived in the northland for thirteen years when they arrived in Iditarod. But after all this time, their father had still not struck it rich. In Iditarod he found work at a dredge mine on Flat Creek, 20 miles from town.

Mrs. McDonald's days of picking berries and baking bread to feed the family were finally over. Her dream of owning a business was appearing before their very eyes. Soon their tent was replaced by a wood-frame building proudly named the McDonald Hotel. Every day it was filled with hungry and tired prospectors hoping to hit pay dirt at the new gold strike. The children helped their mother run the hotel. She also nursed the sick in town. The men called her "Doc" McDonald. In the summer, Sigrid and Donald fished in the nearby creeks, picked wildflowers

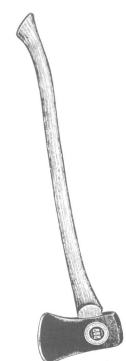

Donald McDonald

on the tundra hills, and played in the street. There were twice as many dogs as people, and they made a racket morning and night. But those very dogs were worth their weight in gold, for they pulled freight to the nearby mining creeks.

When fall arrived, Donald and Sigrid attended school at a one-room schoolhouse. In October, when the streets and nearby hills were covered with snow, they went sledding with their friends. But as temperatures dropped to 50 below or more, they stayed inside reading and listening to records on the Victrola. Donald cut and hauled wood every day to keep the hotel warm.

After the long, cold winter, the children looked forward to springtime in May,

(above) Donald studies at home in his mother's Iditarod hotel.

(right) Sigrid and friends at Iditarod

Children of the Gold Rush

Iditarod was a thriving supply center after gold was discovered in June 1910. But by 1914, the once thriving population of 2000 had dwindled to just 500.

when the snowdrifts melted. They donned their boots and played for hours in the muddy streets. Finally, the water began to run in the creeks and the frozen Innoko River ice melted. Donald, Sigrid, and nearly the entire town population rushed down to meet the first boat of the season. They watched as supplies were unloaded, hoping for some candy, and picked up mail from their relatives.

As he grew older, Donald discovered ways to make money. He collected the Seattle and San Francisco newspapers when they came off the boat. Even though they were months out-of-date, he sold them for $1 and sometimes even earned a tip. The biggest tippers were the pretty dancehall girls who lived on the hill. His mother disliked them, but Donald thought they were some of the nicest people in town. He also delivered telegrams for $1 apiece. Sometimes the prospectors paid him with gold dust.

When the fish ran in the summer, Donald and a partner caught grayling, pike, salmon, and trout in the river and rushed to the restaurants to sell them.

Donald saved most of his money, and

"I remember grabbing handfuls of the biggest and shiniest nuggets.... By the time my parents took me away from Iditarod, I was richer by approximately $5,000 in choice nuggets."

—"I Remember Iditarod," *Alaska Sportsman*, **September 1969**

Iditarod Area

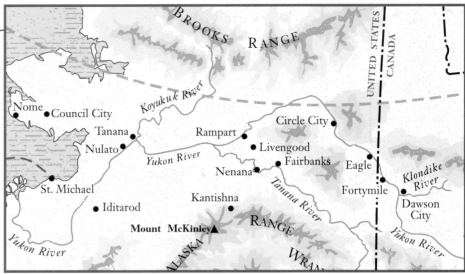

(left) "Little Wonder" phonograph

(below) Gold engraved watch

Donald and Sigrid look out over Iditarod on their way home from school.

sometimes took Sigrid to the candy store or soda pop bottling plant on Main Street for a treat.

Fall brought the most exciting event of the whole year: cleanup. The miners washed the gold from their claims in long sluice boxes. This was Donald and Sigrid's favorite time to visit their father. One of the miners would hoist Donald up into a sluice box and let him help himself to some gold. Donald dipped his hands into the ice-cold water, and his fingers became so numb that he could hardly move them. Still, he managed to grab some nuggets. By 1916, the gold boom in Iditarod was finished. With the money they had made,

Donald, his mother, and Sigrid moved to California to live with relatives. Two years later, Donald's father quit prospecting and left the Northland to join the family. Unfortunately, his ship, the *Princess Sophia*, grounded on a rock near Juneau and sank. All 350 passengers and crew drowned. It was one of the greatest tragedies of the northern gold rushes.

Donald McDonald had experienced both the good and the bad times of boomtown life and had learned to work hard. He grew up to become a successful businessman in California, and like many gold rush children, he wrote about his early adventures in the North.

"Baldy of Nome."
"Scotty" Allen's famous Leader.
Winner of $25,000.00 in Sweepstake prizes.
© Winter & Pond Co.

Beloved Dogs

(top left) Sled dogs like Baldy were famous characters in gold rush Nome, where the Annual Sweepstakes Race was a major event.

(below left) Nero, a St. Bernard, belonged to Belinda Mulrooney, the wealthiest woman in Dawson City. Some people said he served as a model for "Buck" in Jack London's *Call of the Wild*.

(below right) Murphy, like many dogs in the North, helped carry supplies for his owner.

Pack trains depart Dawson for
the gold creeks, 1899.

Washday in Alaska—June 28, 1910

EPILOGUE

Gold rush children learned how to work hard and to make the best of their difficult lives. Whether or not they realized it at the time, they enjoyed the uniqueness of their lives—lives that were very different from those of other children. They met and played with children of many cultures, particularly Native cultures. This gave them an understanding of other people that many Americans did not have. Separation and divorce were common in gold rush families. And some kids were left behind by fathers who took off alone for the Northland, perhaps never to return. Many of these men sent not even a penny home.

Like children all over the world, the young people of the northern gold rushes grew up during a period of tremendous change. By the time they were adults, the telephone, telegraph, and airplane had not only been invented, but were part of everyday life. These inventions profoundly changed life in the North because they provided greater communication with the outside world. Never again would people take off for a gold rush in such great numbers or with such optimism and innocence.

Men, women, and dogs pose in front of the Caribou Hotel, a meeting point and freight stop on one of the creeks outside Dawson. The hotel is built of rough logs chinked with moss, and the roof is made of poles covered with sod.

GLOSSARY

above: A numbering system for mining claims that refers to claims upstream from the discovery, as in "1 above."

Athabascan: A Native Indian group made up of many different bands, living in interior Alaska and the Yukon territories and speaking eleven separate languages.

aurora borealis: (northern lights) Nocturnal shimmering green, blue, white, red, and purple lights caused by charged particles energized by the sun.

below: A numbering system for mining claims that refers to claims downstream from the discovery, as in "80 below."

claim: A plot of ground staked by a miner on which he can mine, usually 660 feet wide and 1,320 feet long.

discovery claim: The first claim on a creek, staked to include the point of discovery of the gold or other mineral.

dredge: A large industrial machine that digs out the gold or other minerals buried in the rock.

drift: The horizontal tunnel dug out to follow the vein of gold at the bottom of the mining shaft.

gold pan: A large, flat pan in which miners and prospectors wash gravel to look for gold.

hard rock claim: A hillside claim staked in a lode deposit.

hard rock gold or lode gold: Mineral deposits encased in surrounding rock in the hillside, must be crushed and refined to free the gold.

midnight sun: The summer sun as seen above the horizon at night above the Arctic Circle.

mushing: traveling with a dog team and sled.

ore: A rock containing valuable minerals.

Outside: anywhere outside of Alaska and the Yukon territory.

panning: The process of washing gravel or crushed rock to separate out gold flakes.

pay dirt: The vein or pocket of dirt containing gold.

paystreak: An underground channel with large amounts of gold, found by sinking a shaft or by drilling from the surface.

placer claims: The claims on a creek where loose gold dust and nuggets are found in buried gravel deposits.

placer gold: Gold found in the gravels of streambeds (adapted from the Spanish word *placel*, meaning "sandbank").

poke: A small moosehide bag used to store gold dust.

potlatch: A Native celebration of dancing and gift-giving to commemorate a special occasion.

recording a claim: After staking, the miner had to travel to the recorder's office where the recorder wrote down a legal description of the claim location and the miner filed a copy of the location notice

riffles: Small sticks or boards nailed across the bottom of the sluice box to catch the heavy gold particles as the gravel is washed out of the box.

riverboat: A large sternwheel or paddle-wheel vessel powered by steam.

rocker: A small semi-portable gold-washing device consisting of a screen, and slanted wash box. The box-like device is on rockers like a rocking chair. Water is scooped into the box and the box is rocked with a handle to shake the gravel and wash it away, leaving the gold.

scow: A large, flat, bargelike boat made out of sawed lumber.

shaft: A vertical hole dug down to bedrock on a placer or hard rock claim.

sluice box: A long, narrow wooden box about 16 inches wide, 12 inches deep, and 20 feet long or more, used to wash out the gold from the gravel on a placer claim.

smelter: A large factory where ore is reduced in a furnace to separate out metals from the rock.

sourdough: Naturally fermented yeast carried by pioneers to leaven bread and pancakes.

staking a claim: Marking the corners of a mining claim according to rules of the mining district and filling out and posting a location notice.

trading post: An isolated frontier store where goods were traded, bartered or sold.

tunnel: A horizontal hole dug into the bedrock of a hillside to look for minerals.

Children of the Gold Rush

FURTHER READING

Assorted authors. "The Klondike Stampede" of 1897–1898 in the *Cobblestone Magazine* (August 1989). Peterborough, NH: Cobblestone Publishing.

Cooper, Michael. *Klondike Fever: the Famous Gold Rush of 1898*. New York: Clarion Books, 1989.

Declements, Barth. *The Bite of the Gold Bug*. New York: Penguin Books, 1992.

Dodson, Peggy Rouch. *Girl of the Gold Camp*. Fairbanks/Seattle: Epicenter Press, co-published by Beistline Enterprises, 1996.

Griese, Arnold. *Anna's Athabascan Summer*. Honesdale, PA: Boyds Mills Books, 1995.

Hughes, Monica. *Gold Fever Trail*. Toronto: Panda Books, General Paperbacks, 1990.

Murphy, Claire Rudolf, and Jane G. Haigh. *Gold Rush Women*. Anchorage, Seattle, Portland: Alaska Northwest Books, 1997.

Nelson, Klondy, with Corey Ford. *Daughter of the Gold Rush*. New York: Random House, 1958.

Ray, Delia. *Gold: The Klondike Adventure*. New York, NY: Lodestar Books, 1989.

Neufeld, David and Frank Norris. *Chilkoot Trail: Heritage Route to the Klondike*. Whitehorse: Lost Moose, the Yukon Publishers, 1996.

Wold, Jo Anne. *The Way It Was*. Anchorage: Alaska Northwest Books, 1978.

SOURCES

The Snow Family Collection at the Alaska State Library contains family photographs and Crystal's stories, poems, songs, and letters. Sources on the Cherosky family are obscure, so we are grateful to family members. Ethel Anderson Becker's story is told in her article "Little Girl in the Klondike Goldfields," *Alaska Sportsman*, November 1962, and also her book, *A Treasury of Alaskana*, New York, Superior Publishing Co., 1969. For information about the Moore family, we are grateful to an unpublished paper by Doreen Cooper, Project Archeologist at the Klondike Gold Rush National Historic Park in Skagway and J. Bernard Moore's book, *Skagway in Days Primeval: Diary and Recollections of J. Bernard Moore, 1865-1919*, Lynn Canal Publishing Company, 1997. Robert Farnsworth's unpublished memoir is in his collection at the University of Alaska Fairbanks archives, and also excerpted in "An Army Brat Goes to Alaska," *Alaska Journal*, volumes 3 and 4, 1977. For Antoinette and Annette Mayo's story, we are grateful to descendant Barbara Nelson. Klondy Nelson Dufresne's memoir, *Daughter of the Gold Rush*, Random House, 1958, is a classic. Jo Anne Wold told Cleora Casady Bachner's story in her book *The Way It Was*, Anchorage, Alaska Northwest Publishing, 1978, and we used Cleora's complete unpublished manuscript. Vide Bartlett's story is told in Claus Naske's biography of her husband, *E. L. Bob Bartlett of Alaska: A Life in Politics*, University of Alaska Press, 1979. A tantalizing memoir by Donald McDonald's mother Alice, "As Well as Any Man," in *Alaska Journal*, Summer 1984, attracted our attention to her story. Donald also published a memoir in *Alaska Sportsman*, "I Remember Iditarod," September 1969.

PHOTO CREDITS